Memories and Imaginations

Tiàrnan McGarrity

Memories, Musings and Imaginations ©
2023 Tiàrnan McGarrity

All rights reserved.

No part of this publication may be
reproduced, stored in a retrieval system, or
transmitted, in any form or by any means,
electronic, mechanical, photocopying,
recording or otherwise, without the prior
written permission of the presenters.

Tiàrnan McGarrity asserts the moral right
to be identified as author of this work.

Presentation by *BookLeaf Publishing*

Web: www.bookleafpub.com

E-mail: info@bookleafpub.com

ISBN: 9789357696784

First edition 2023

DEDICATION

This book is dedicated to my twin from another kin, Zara Jackson, whose patience, understanding, and love, knows no bounds.

PREFACE

I've been more of a songwriter than a poet over the years, but the reasons for my interest in poetry and music overlap, both can entertain, transport and distract you, make you feel something, think something, that you hadn't necessarily felt or thought before. All poetry comes from the heart, but the same can't be said for all music.

I have a small collection of poetry books, my favourite of which is simply entitled, "Zen Poems," some of the content of which has made me feel a connection with a person who lived more than 1000 years ago, which is really something that speaks to the power of poetry, and to its importance.

I feel like there's a chance now, however slim, that in 50 or 60 years or more, someone will find a dilapidated copy of this book in a thrift store, pay the 25p (or economic equivalent at that time, probably a far greater value...), and have a similar experience. Doesn't matter what it is, whatever paragraph or sentence or sentiment that makes sense, even if it's just one thing, I'll consider this whole endeavour a roaring success. I've always found the arts to be a refuge, as many do, and to be a part of that grand legacy, would be a great honour. Through connection we grow, we develop, we learn the value of striving for others.

This sheds some light on my reasons for writing this book (apart from wanting to shake up the personal status quo and challenge/scare myself); times are tough, and I've come to realise that they always have been, which is of tremendous relief to realise. Think of your worst day ever. You got through it, no bother. The rest of this is just here for us to enjoy, no matter what happens. Just thought I'd share that positive note with you before you read on into the utterly daunting material that is to follow...and on that note;

I hope that something from the following pages will ring true, entertain, or aid you in your own life and battles, reader, for it has certainly been an aid to me, to write of them.

Moments in Time

They often seem to slip us by,
The gravity of a situation or a said word,
Seems to increase,
The further you travel from it.

All too quickly, our lives pass by,
Dwelling on missed opportunities,
What you should have said,
What you should have done.

If you're not careful,
The opportunities of the future,
Can be lost,
In the fog of the past.

A cacophony of not quite's,
Almost's and if only's,
Cascading down,
Towards that place.

It can make one seek destruction,
But equally,
It can make one seek redemption,
If only,
It could make one find peace.

Being fully present,
In the moment,
Will usually prevent such demons.

A Starling Glides

The sky, as vast as infinity,
today the clouds seem to be also,
but this is an illusion.

Overhead, a Starling glides,
with no care for far away thoughts.

Back Home From France

I turn the corner,
see you reading through the window.
Relief hits me
like a focusing lens
magnifying the moment.
I walk in.
Eyes lock,
ablaze with anticipation.
Softly spoken words come forth
and strike like thunder.
The atmosphere condenses,
as the gravity between us increases.
The distance closes.
Your hand strokes my arm,
sending waves across the universe.
Giddy laughter ensues.
We embrace.
Your lips brush my ear,
emanating a soft sigh,
as Pharaohs of the ancient world
lay abandoned
at your Feet.

Some Days

Some days prick the skin,
like a cactus needle,
the hurt only felt when it's alright deep in.
A sudden sharp jolt followed by realisation.
If only fear and doubt,
were as easy to remove.

Some days chill the bones,
gather dust and rust,
seem to stretch on for eternity.
The regret of inaction sets in as the moon rises.
"If only I had've done more"
we all chant in unison.

Some days hit hard,
like a sledgehammer to the chest.
All breath seemingly vanishes.
Good choices can diminish those experienced,
in number,
But such days are inevitable.

Some days weigh heavy.
Atmosphere of a raised viscosity,
world on the shoulders.
Something as simple as remembering to smile,

conjures with it notions,
of Sisyphus.

Some days.
Some days are a revelation,
A delivery from the ruined pathways,
Yesterday is done and gone,
Today begins anew,
And tomorrow never comes.

Some days suck.

I'm grateful that today doesn't.

Neuronic Fire

Rapid vapid rushes cause blushes to reek from cheeks top and bottom, though under different circumstances.

Vastly costly viaducts run out of luck and crash like smashed eggplants, spilling water and wasting life.

Surprise uprisings unwisely cast sizeable and undeniable shadows, across the field of its intended crop.

Hurry worry worts there's all sorts of dreams bathing upstream, but you'll never get there by swimming.

Exalted haunted heirlooms in bedrooms move silently yet violently about, causing confusion and unrest in the living.

Pricey sliced rice on ice won't feed your nutritional needs, but some still pay for it if it's dressed right.

Waving brave slaves crowd perilous caves willingly for a chance to join the dance, knowing the rocks could fall any minute.

Tired wired firecrackers sullenly sit and grow their emanations of woe, all in the name of understanding do they suffer.

The Orchestration

It's all around us,
Whether or not it can be heard,
It's in the days first light,
It's in those three little words,
In the shade of a tree,
The thought of a lie,
The death of a lover,
It's in that look,
In your eye.

It makes the strain,
And the breath pass by,
Without it there wouldn't be,
Any life or earth, any stars or sky
It brings order to the chaos,
Within the score,
Form and structure reside,
Without it there would be madness,
A hollow cave,
That's solid inside.

Countless forms in harmony,
Playing unrehearsed,
Exploring the colour and timbre,
Of this Aeolin Universe,

Each beat keeping in time,
With the rhythm of dying Black Holes,
Each note perfectly voiced,
As the orchestration flows.

Each chord held together,
Inversions cartwheel along the stream,
Each measure fully realised,
Every tone chimes crisp and clean,
Each string perfectly played,
Plucked by hands unseen,
On the instrumental fabric,
Of what is awake,
Within the dream.

Summer Dress

The mid-day sun pours across the glistening
hillside as odd spots of speckled cloud shadow
lazily meander along.

People all around the lower fields and upper
pathways are basking and strolling, playing
games and singing songs.

Birds fly from tree-top to tree-top securing their
territories perimeter, engaging in arguments and
shouting distress.

A fitting tone to a beautiful memory,

of a girl in a summer dress.

A spark that came to life among the riotous
Saturday night city club scene, flaming much
laughter

and future love making.

A spark given fuel through a chance encounter
in the market square, that lead to much love

and future heart break.

Memories of this time are more than hazy as if
viewed through frosted glass,

each kiss, caress.

Over the years that have gone by much has been
lost and forgotten,

but not the summer dress.

Rain clouds smoother the sky in a featureless
haze as buildings and cars are bathed in the drab
grey light of monotony.

Early afternoon hustles and bustles about at
different speeds and temperatures but all serve
the same ideology.

A planned encounter has just taken place,
reluctant goodbyes leave hearts racing, minds a
mess,

a boy left standing

waving goodbye,

to the girl

in the summer dress.

Slightly Less Depressed-ly

Slightly less depressed-ly,
is a good way to go.
It's far from ecstatic,
as you rightly know.
It's a kind of inward outlook,
that can get you through the day,
if you're more or less used,
to not getting your way.

Slightly less depressed-ly,
it's not hard to do.
A certain melancholy perception,
an odd kind of view.
It doesn't take much effort,
to raise your mood a little,
when it's often found that happiness,
is all too weak and brittle.

Slightly less depressed-ly,

Oh no,

I appear to be making a scene.

No one cares if you're in pain,

when your face looks so obscene.
All they see is the unknown element,
breaking down before their eyes.
All they want to do is be rid of it,
which comes to me as no surprise.

They say,

"Sure knowing is half the battle."

And,

"What's meant for you won't pass you by."

But what I've known
has been cause
for surrender.

Any fate,
unwillingly defied.

I've paid too much attention,
to the hatred and the lies,

But slightly less depressed-ly,
here's some advice to live by;

Carry yourself
tall,

Keep your chin
high,
Practice morning
mantras,
Just believe
the lie,
Keep the smile
un-wooden,
Blink the tears
from your eyes,
Still the foaming
mind-scape,
Mute the deepening
sighs,
Be honest
with your heart,
Allow yourself
to cry,
Surrender to the fact,
that all that lives
will one day die.
Know your greatest enemy
lives within,
deep inside.

Genetic Echoes

Prevalent,
hard to master.
Easier to handle
one day at a time.

A set of unelected traits.
A handout varying in utility.
Instruction manual vague,
often missing.

A curse and
a blessing,
though one is easier to see
than the other.

A state of flux,
mixing what is desired,
what is pre-written,
and what could be.

The true reality;
That to which we're exposed
over time
is engraved and transmuted
into the core of our being.

Silent Treatment

Mind fractured,
heart,
schism'd.
News,
not taken well,
reeks of a mistake.

Days pass,
no word,
wits end.
A letter written,
delivered by hand,
to reassurances.

Then,
nothing,
but
slow rot,
ghostly encounters,
deepening fear.

It stays with you,
prevalently,
being ignored
willfully

by someone
you love.

A bitter well
excavated
by careless hands.
Dug too deep
without
much forethought.

Within,
ideas of
worthlessness,
self-loathing,
disgust,
careen giddily.

The compulsion
to act,
coupled,
with the inability
to convey.
The perfect storm.

A betrayal
by internal
forces,
that persist,
and demand,

and gnaw.

The wound,
though healed,
still weeps,
at times.
It's hard
not to worry it.

Self-worth,
no longer
an alien concept,
but still faded,
worn out,
indifferent.

It is akin
to a death,
this silent treatment,
The absence
so sudden,
and purposeful.

It is akin
to a death.

Only the one who you grieve,
is sometimes seen,
running in the opposite direction.

Or they're sat across the way,
drunk and obscene,
proclaiming their love to strangers.

Or they're telling a sad tale,
to all who will listen,
of a strange man,
and a letter written.

A letter spilled out
in fearful haste,
a jumbled convolution,
poorly paced.

A disgusting treaty
out of time,
that transformed into
its own punchline.

A joke bestowed
for all to enjoy,
a joke bestowed
of a man destroyed.

A joke bestowed
for all to jeer.

Yet still, I pleaded

upon deaf ears.

In denial, the message
made more than clear.

We're all too damaged
these days, I fear.

The Spider

The Spider sat beside her weaving tales of
deceit,
the weaving never stopping for an instance or a
heartbeat.
Here and there she spied the subtle tells of a lie,
but never did she waver from his hypnotic eyes.

Until,

the tells and inklings could no longer be
ignored,
the vibrations of the lies had harmonised and
struck a chord,
So she tried to run, but found her body stuck
in place,
As the silken fibres strained against her
limbs, she's face to face

with The Spider.

Who, now within an inch and weaving still,
at last his fangs exposed,
goes in for the kill.

The Spotlight Effect

They're all looking at me.
A sea of faces of every disposition.
Studying every detail.
Eyes catch the more sneerful glares,
ignoring those of optimism.

"How's it going?"

The pre-rehearsed intro dialogue begins, but
doubt creeps in before mumbling off.

"Anyway! Here we go."

The guitar puts up a fight, pressured fingers
sweat tension trying to keep it in check, it must
be holding a grudge from the last time.
Microphone seems to change its mind as to
what distance it prefers, and is definitely
amplifying inaccuracies out of spite.
Notes, just barely hit, pass through an ever
tiring tongue whose dance, though well
rehearsed, fails to find the right rhythm.
A vocal crack, due to not breathing properly,
echoes around the room before backslapping
redness into more faces than just my own.

"Alright that's me, thank you!"

 The odd spattered bit of empathetic applause
breaks through the wall of conversation,
as weakened legs shuffle ego off the stage,
seeking some drink or substance,
to release the body.

Running at Night

Street lights pass by at a slow and purposely
jaunt, illuminating the path ahead.

The town's half empty, pass by a few people,
more can be seen in the bar, and takeaways.

The odd surge of traffic passes by, tweaking
interest in the occupants, their story.

Some have a right ole stare as they pass,
no doubt thinking, "look at him, dick."

Many's the night when I'd have been crawling
home drunk, but that time has largely passed,
resigned to the holidays and odd birthday.

Jagged memories shift uncomfortably as they
are disturbed from their slumber, majority coated
in moss, malnourished, but still strong enough to
fuel the body, and promote extra speed and
focus.

Until they, and their influence, pass by, and the
body is left in shock, pace slowed to a half step.

It's not long before the system returns to normal, breathing becomes less strained, and the pain passes by.

Eventually, everything passes by.

What's He Listening To?

Kendrick righteously rapping
about the state of the people,
dying of thirst but united in grief

Joshua singing sweetly
about the only thing he fears (himself),
and his want to not die sober

Maynard prolifically preaching
about sour grapes and Jesus,
10,000 days in the fire is long enough

Ian repeatedly reminding us to
forgive everybody and remember,
for everything, a reason

Chris adamantly admitting
to wallowing in the mud and blood
on the day he tried to live

Hope consciously confessing
to wanting to keep love away,
to knowing

John lazily lamenting

about the comedy of man
and his place in the universe

Robert wickedly wailing
about the woes of life
since he's been loving you

Josh cantankerously crooning
about the pitfalls of love,
how one can disappear

There are many other names,
that could be added to this list.
I'm tempted to add and add and add,
but this temptation, I will resist.

For this list alone suffices,
in proving something base.
The songs may be from different genres,
but they're all born of the human race.

Pain and strife and longing and woe,
weaved through rhythm, base and melody.
People just trying to make sense of it all,
etched forever in sonic memory.

Under These Stars

I've sat under these stars for many long nights,
gazing with wonder at the soft streaming lights,
the darker it grows, the more they shine bright,
giving hope to those who need it.

With a yawn and a sigh I stand up to leave,
the wind carries a whisper, hands clasp at my
sleeve,
I turn to yell but forget how to breathe,
for the sight is enough to unman me.

As I look in her eyes my mind starts to race,
and try as I might I can't stop the pace,
I look down ashamed, tears spill on my face,
because now, I know I am dreaming.

She leans in close to offer a kiss,
her lips are as soft as gentle sweet bliss,
my mind is consumed by the one that I miss,
as my eyes open wide to the darkness.

As I lie here alone I think of the past,
of how I thought that forever we'd last,
but time flew by, ever so fast,
how I wish I had cherished every moment.

I've sat under these stars for many long nights,
my gaze now blind to the soft streaming lights,
down on the ground, seeking respite,
from regrets, and imperfect memories.

An Evening at Boulder World

Chalked hands,
chapped and rough,
fingers taped
where the skin has failed.

Clothing sparse
to allow free movement,
toes huddled together
in skin tight shoes.

A mixture of ability levels,
strength on display from all,
greenhorns and veterans alike
all striving to be better.

The local experts
are a sight to behold,
gracefully and with ease,
do they produce the impossible.

Conversation sparks
between strangers
as support is given by those
tackling the same problem.

Challenging routes,
bravely challenged,
with gleeful impatience
and excitable apprehension.

Across the hall,
a hushed cheer emanates,
as a small group celebrates,
their friends successful climb.

The Nearly Men

We were quite the pair,
I was a ruffled loose end,
You were a sharp dressed beginning.
It's interesting, how we were painted with the
same brush.
Both storytellers, but maybe, one too many
stories told,
at our own expense.
The shared ability to turn an unpleasant
or embarrassing experience,
into a piece of Saturday night live stand up,
delivering riotous laughter,
but reinforcing the merit of failure,
consecrating the vicious cycle.
It was all too late when I realised,
for years have disappeared,
and contact has been lost.

But now I say to you;

To Hell with Pavlov,
I decree, the end of it.
The Nearly Men are no more.
I remove the moniker,
liquidate its platinum plaque,

and strip away its power.
I free the lands under its wrath,
illuminate the darkened pathways,
and nourish the dusty soil.
I release the unjustly imprisoned beliefs,
resurrect the abandoned industries,
and cast aside any leftover harvest.

I tell you,
the legacy was false.
The prophecy untrue.
The moment is yours to take.
Absolved, you are,
Brand New.

Her Earth

Her earth has moved beneath me,
I've scaled the mountain peaks,
swam in turquoise waters,
for the answer there to seek.

I've walked her arid desert,
arrived on golden shores,
slept beside her sheltered heart,
never wanting more.

I've basked out in her summer sun,
her winter, I have fought,
but nothing ever led me to
the answers I had sought.

Always they eluded me,
and they will forever more,
for soon I found her earth replaced,
by dread, and the cold, barren floor.

Now I walk this empty land,
my empathy near spent,
longing for her earth, which,
all to quickly, came and went.

Diving In

Ice cold water flows rhythmically over panicked feet, grey-blue undulations stretch on far beyond the horizon.

Shins protest as they are forced to take another cautious step forward, but they hold little sway.

Submerging the knees isn't bad at all, they can even be quite welcoming, but it only gets tougher from there.

Thighs and groin are persuaded without too much effort, but the gut is too good a debator at times, and don't even get me started on the heart.

My tactic is usually to slowly walk in up to my waist, take five deep breaths, then dive, but this isn't always the case.

There are times I have ran and jumped in, other times where the number of breaths taken is closer to thirty-five than five, and even the rare times where, in a grand political upheaval, the thighs protestations cause too much concern for the establishment, who then see clear to cancel the event.

Not today though.

Today, it's all hands on deck, fire the engines, set course along the coastline.

Prepare to submerge.

Now rejoice! For the land and the woes it holds are left behind this day, the cold abysmal void opens its warm embrace to us, so that we may be tested, tempered, and baptized anew, by that from which we came.

I arrive back at the car, and take a moment to reflect on the experience, laughing at the joyful discomfort of it, and revelling in a reinvigorated gratitude for warm clothes, shelter, and life.

The Beast Tiberius

The early morning sun skims the overgrown tree-tops as various varieties of garden birds harmonise excitably back and forth, spreading gossip and arguing about breakfast, as they revel in the promise of a new day.

I'm on my third distasteful smoke and second bitter coffee, but it's alright. The wild beast, Tiberius, black and gold striped, with claws for paws and dagger sharp grin, sits to my left, half ready to pounce at the sky.

He's at war, you see. Everyday, the skirmishes begin anew. He doesn't seem to mind the smaller birds, even letting them dance around him, or congregate at his food bowl, but only when he thinks nobody's looking.

The Wood-Pigeons, Blackbirds, Magpies, Crows and Seagulls though, are all on the kill list. He has caught a good few, through stealth and agility, which is disconcerting for a creature of his size. He is mercifully swift.

Suddenly he bolts for the far hedge, low growl emanating, before catapulting himself through the air with a war cry, and punctuating a large full-stop through the foliage, where seconds ago, a vengeful Blackbirds beady eye glared.

The birds reasons for war are clear, having lost a mate in the fray. Tiberius' reasons, most likely, stem from the work of carrion birds, witnessed, perhaps fought off, during his unfortunate youth, speculative as that may be.

He always has a reason. Anytime we've fought, I've realised on reflection that I escalated the situation. He is made of buttery toast and scritches, when he feels safe. Fear and anxiety make the raw meat and torn tissue come out.

He returns from the punctured hedgerow, unsuccessful and disappointed, head slightly bowed, licking his lips, expectant of reassurance. I scratch his ear and offer him a favourite treat, which he politely accepts.

Let That Be It

Let that be it
release this wretched heart
wring your hands of it
hold them high and proclaim
"I am innocent of this blood"
and let that be it

Milton Keynes UK
Ingram Content Group UK Ltd.
UKHW020842250823
427479UK00016B/577